숨

숨

장훈 디카시집

두엄

시인의 말
(A Poet's Note)

세상의 모든 움직임을 멈춰 세워,
그 안에 숨겨진 이야기를 들춰봅니다.
이름 없는 몸짓에 이름을 불러 꽃 피우듯,
작고 소외된 것들에 끝없는 관심을 두고
찰나의 순간을 영원한 시로 만드는 것이
제게 던져진 과제이자,
숨이 붙어 있는 동안 계속될 천상의 행군입니다.

I halt every motion of the world,
and delve into the stories hidden within.
Like giving names to nameless gestures, making them bloom,
I pour endless attention onto the small and the overlooked.
To transform fleeting moments into eternal verse—
this is the task cast upon me,
a celestial march that will endure as long as breath remains.

차례

1부

웃음사슬 · 14
스마일 바이러스 · 15
굴뚝 웃음 · 16
웃음꽃 · 17
오독 · 18
사월의 풍등 · 19
삼랑진 철교 · 20
더운갈이꽃 · 21
어머니의 샘터 · 22
골목길의 온도 · 23
봄비 내리는 날 · 24
알츠하이머 · 25
기념사진 · 26
아름다운 주정 · 27
관상목 자서전 · 28
채석강 · 29
파도의 노래 · 30
기도의 속도 · 31
발자국 · 32
벗의 유혹 · 33

봄의 좌표 · 34

어떤 화해 · 35

초자아 · 36

춘정(春情) · 37

독백 · 38

안간힘 · 39

노루막이 · 40

막대인간 · 41

상한가 연정 · 42

협심증 · 43

쌈짓골 노병 · 44

흰머리 청춘 · 45

미안해요 · 46

바람벽 · 47

동행 · 48

반작용 · 49

부부 · 50

부부송의 전설 · 51

첫사랑 · 52

신혼 · 53

폐경 · 54

한낮한시 · 55
숨 · 56
경청 · 57
뒤돈 화살표 · 58
내가 만난 둘리 · 59
상선약수에 사족을 달다 · 60
이념의 강 · 61
유산 · 62
용서 · 63
겨울을 맛있게 먹는 법 · 64
나의 영토 · 65
비행 청소년 · 66
사계만정 · 67
사춘기 · 68
성급한 테크놀러지 · 69
수호자 · 70
유튜버 · 71
취준생 · 72
살살이꽃 · 73
대나무처럼 · 74
헤테로토피아 · 75

2부

Chain of Laughter · 78

Smile Virus · 79

Chimney's Laughter · 80

Laughter Blooms · 81

Misjudgment · 82

April's Sky Lanterns · 83

Samrangjin Iron Bridge · 84

Spring's Arduous Tilling Flower · 85

Mother's Spring · 86

The Alley's Temperature · 87

On a Rainy Spring Day · 88

Alzheimer's · 89

Commemorative Photo · 90

Beautiful Drunken Reverie · 91

Autobiography of an Ornamental Tree · 92

Chaeseokgang · 93

Song of the Waves · 94

The Speed of Prayer · 95

Footprint · 96

The Allure of the Cherry Blossom · 97

Coordinates of Spring · 98

A Certain Reconciliation · 99

Superego · 100

Spring's Stirrings · 101

Monologue · 102

The Struggle · 103

The Roe Deer's Halt · 104

A conduit's life · 105

Upper Limit Yearning · 106

Angina · 107

The Old Soldier of Ssamjitgol · 108

White-Haired Youth · 109

I'm Sorry · 110

Wind Wall · 111

Together · 112

Counteraction · 113

Couple · 114

The Legend of the Couple Pine Tree · 115

First Love · 116

Newlywed · 117

Menopause · 118

Same Day, Same Hour · 119

Breath · 120

Listening · 121

A Backward Arrow · 122

The Dooly I Met · 123

Adding a Footnote to "The Highest Good is Like Water" · 124

The River of Ideologies · 125

Legacy · 126

Forgiveness · 127

How to Savor Winter · 128

My Territory · 129

Flying Youth · 130

Everlasting Affection · 131

Adolescence · 132

Impatient Technology · 133

Guardian · 134

You Tuber · 135

Job seeker · 136

Salsal-i Flower (Cosmos) · 137

Like bamboo, · 138

Heterotopia · 139

1부

웃음사슬

웃음은 최상위 포식자, 천적이 없다

세상살이 찌든 때 한 입에 다 삼켜버려

스마일 바이러스

전염시켜 줄까
빗방울도 웃게 만드는
지독한 유전자야

젖은 마음을 말리는 데는
이만한 게 없어

굴뚝 웃음

제 가슴에 뜨거운 불을 지필 때마다
주름이 한 칸씩 늘었나요

숯검정 같은 속사정
하얗게 태우시던 아버지 감투

웃음꽃

해맑은 말들이
맛있게 쏟아지는 점심시간
복도 끝까지 굴러가 환하게 핀다

어른들이 귓등으로도 못 담을 만큼

오독

빈 깡통처럼 소리만 셈한다고
누더기를 입었다고
하품하는 넝마라 하더군

내 주변이 온통 꽃인 줄 모르고

사월의 풍등

오래 껴안고

오래 울었습니다

삼랑진 철교

소 끌고 삼십 리 길
쇠심줄 다리였던 아버지

지팡이를 짚고도
끝내 멈추지 않고
저 강을 다 건너셨다

더운갈이꽃

봄나물이 가물면 당신 마음도 말라진다고
땅이 슬도록 넘나들어 허리 굽은 어머니
한사코 자투리에서도 더운갈이하시는

어머니의 샘터

슬픔조차 마중물로 헹구시던 당신 말씀,

한여름 냉수와 같이 쏟아지네

골목길의 온도

해 떨어진 게 언젠데 밥 먹으러 안 오냐
어머니의 고함소리가 달라 붙은 담벼락
줄어든 키만큼
사람들의 온기는 식어가고 있었다

봄비 내리는 날

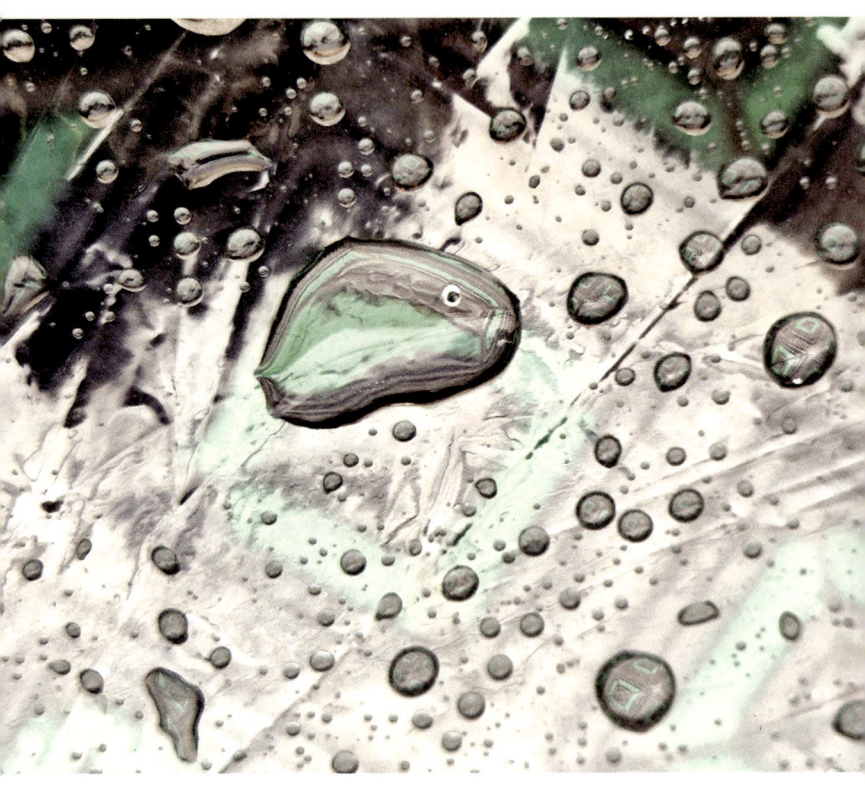

빗방울이 머무는 동안
세상은 아쿠아리움인데

우산은 기울기의 슬픔을 안다

당신이 떠난 봄날의 끝에
내 속으로도 내리는 방울들

알츠하이머

살다 보니 기억이 잘 안나
별별 길을 다 지나왔어
헌 집 받고 새 집 준 것 같은데
탄탄대로는 분명 아니야

기념사진

마른 얼굴에
가을 주름이 늘어가는구나

천둥 번개쯤
눈 하나 꿈쩍 않고
살아왔는데

아름다운 주정

일어나자 친구야
별도 저문 새벽이다

우리 밤새워 마신들
네 속 젖은 아픔
달랠 길 있으랴

관상목 자서전

당신께 위로여서 새순을 피웠을까
눈 안에 저를 담아 시린 속도 읽어주길
책장 속 잠언처럼 서 있다

채석강

관절이 삐거덕거리도록
빗장을 걸었다
그래도 드러나는
속마음을 어찌할까

바다는 참…

파도의 노래

수많은 사연이 모래밭에 쌓이면
바다는 절여진 문장을 엽서체로 내민다

반으로 접힌 노래 행간은 깊고 넓어
귀로 읽는 갈매기 파도 따라 부른다

기도의 속도

결핍의 단추를 하나씩 꿰어 매는 건
간절하게 옷을 입는 것이어서
나의 기도는 느리지만
멈추지 않아

발자국

시간의 뒤꿈치로
이름표 하나 새겨 놓았나

너 여기서
숨 쉬고 사랑하며
맘껏 뛰놀았다고

벗의 유혹

아, 어쩌란 말인가
봄날엔 꽃잎으로 두근거리게 하더니
가을엔 하늘을 꿰매 입다
단추 하나 떨어뜨리고
속 비친 그대 실루엣

봄의 좌표

고니와 수학이 만나는 순간
행과 열로 좌표가 된 작은 세상

겨울을 휘저으면
물결은 곱셈으로 퍼져나가
푸드득 깃을 쳐야 할 그 자리

어떤 화해

얼마나 검질기게 다투었으면
보다 못한 봄이

겨울과 겨울에게
화해를 청한다

초자아

수백 년 바람을 맞아가며
계절의 옹이를 새겨 놓고

중심에 든 신전

땅속 비밀을 움켜쥔 채
죽어서도 산다

춘정(春情)

혼자 푸른 소나무
아랫도리 간지러운 봄

연분홍 꽃바람에
솔방울 다 놓치겠다

독백

이보게,
인적 없는 곳이라도 적막하지는 않네

빈자리는 햇살이 채워주고
시린 무릎은 담장이 막아주고

바람은 세상 소식 살뜰히 전해준다네

안간힘

침목 하나 넘어가는 일을 두고
앓는 소리 하다간

천국도 지옥이라 할 걸

노루막이

결핍은 허공에도 둥지를 틔운다
슬픔 한 채 얽히듯 기워 놓고
하루치 근육을 단단히 메고 있는,

막대인간

머리는 뜨겁게
가슴은 차갑게
어쩌다 예스맨으로 사는 법

상한가 연정

욕망은 달콤하여 머리꼭지까지 자라지만
뜨겁게 피어오르는 붉은 기둥은 없었다
쫓기듯 엄지를 누르면 시퍼런 부스럼만 남았다
아, 잡을 수 없는 신기루여

협심증

혈관이 터져 나오도록
뒷목 잡는 일이어도

핏발 선 언어를 뱉지 않아야 해

터질 듯 부풀어도
하늘은 열렸으니까

쌈짓골 노병

몸은 늙어서도
새파란 이불을 덮고 있지만
창공을 날아오를 기세나
구름을 뚫고 나갈 깡은
여전해

흰머리 청춘

세월이 눈처럼 내려 무거워졌어도
한때의 초록을 시샘말자

졸고 있는 호수의 뒤통수에
물수제비, 봄을 뜨자

미안해요

내년 봄엔 달라지겠다고
풀반지 하나로 퉁치지 않겠다고
30년을 거짓말하였습니다

바람벽

뒤돌아 자기 말만 하는 아내
나의 잘못을 콕 집어 말해 달라는 남편

보이지 않는 것을 허물려면
마주할 용기가 필요해

동행

여보, 해 떨어져요
같이 있는데 뭘…

등 굽은 노을이
그윽하게 엿듣고 있다

반작용

네가 다가오면 난 아파

철썩일 때마다
붓질매로 맞는 도화지처럼 구겨져
절벽을 세워 얼굴을 바꾸지

달라면 내어주고 밀어내면 버티면서

부부

바람이 매서울 때
우거지는 눈꽃으로
어둠이 무심할 때
다독이는 별빛으로
뜨겁게 보듬어주는 사람

부부송의 전설

벼이삭이 들려주는 풍악소리에 홀려
그림 속으로 들어간 뱃사공 부부
아무리 노를 저어도 나가질 않아
황금 들판에 정박한 나무가 되었다는

첫사랑

사랑은 햇살을 모으는 일
마주치는 순간
온 몸을 열고 싶어

신혼

이불을 펼치기 전 터져 나오는
첫눈처럼 뽀송해

몽글몽글한 생각에
밤을 꼬박 새우는 동안,

폐경

익숙한 어제를 잃어 서러웠을까
붉은 시간 끝자락에 불쑥 찾아온 열기

거울처럼 빛나는 별 둘 다듬어 길렀으니
다시 너를 찾아가는 낯선 진통일 뿐이야

한날한시

허무한 바람이었던가요

담벼락에 쪼그려 앉아
햇살 나누어 먹은 기억이 찬란한데

나는, 조금 더 남아
여기 있네요

숨

구멍 난 폐로 누워있는 산이 되었어도
내쉬는 숨 끝에 처자식의 깍지 낀 기도가 있었고

검정하늘 아래 막장을 오가며 속내를 감추었어도
뜨거운 심장으로 아랫목을 데웠다오

경청

수억 년을 곪고 곪아
쏟아내는 단 한마디

와르르

뒤돈 화살표

길 잃은 곳에서
어디로 가야 할지 모를 때

고집 센 촛대 보다
헝클어져도 물방울처럼

내가 만난 둘리

터널 속에서
더듬거리는 날들이 있었어

그때까진 몰랐었지
내 안에 빛이 있었다는 것을

상선약수*에 사족을 달다

가장 낮은 곳에 머무르며
물 흐르듯 갈까요

맹수의 얼굴을 가진 높은 곳은
두 눈 뜨고 맞설까요

*상선약수(上善若水) : 노자의 도덕경 8장에 나오는 사자성어

이념의 강

난 햇살의 동쪽으로
넌 바람의 서쪽으로

세월의 지느러미에 묶여 있어도
물 들어오면 함께 가는 것을

유산

싹은 틔울 만큼 틔웠고
열매도 맺을 만큼 맺어봤다
지지고 볶고 살아야 할 쓸모는
유산으로 남긴다

용서

어찌 쉬울까
말문을 막아버린 돌덩이
툭, 내려놓으면

길 없는 길도
길이 되어 간다는데

겨울을 맛있게 먹는 법

입맛이 꽁꽁 얼어
녹을 날이 아득할 때

뽀얀 눈가루를 범벅으로 입히고
저온 햇살에 고소하게 튀겨요

어때요, 맛있어 보이나요

나의 영토

휴게소 후미진 정원 한 뼘
수염 곧추 세우고 지켜야지
나는 왕이로소이다

너는 그냥 바쁘게 지나가면 돼

비행 청소년

넌 너대로 빛나니

그냥 날아가면 돼

사계만정

밥손이 닿는 곳은
눈동자도 배부른 자리

사랑은 눈에 담는 거여서
밥 먹으면서도 엄마만 쳐다봐

사춘기

양처럼 순했던 아이는 어디 갔을까

공부해야지 그러면
이제 하려 하는데
왜 그러세요 란다

울타리 밖엔 무엇이 있어 저쪽만 보나

성급한 테크놀러지

어찌할까요?
땅 위를 구르다 하늘을 나는
그날이 온다지만
벌써 이리 올려 두시면

수호자

이봐요 신씨아저씨
뒷동네는 불꽃축제 한창인데

빨간 눈 부릅뜨고
밤새 마을 지키느라
수고 많으십니다

유튜버

동네방네 알리는 일이
참이면 좋겠어

늘어진 땅거미와 사랑을 나누는
바람의 혓바닥처럼

False가 아닌 True

취준생

폭설을 예감하고
바닥의 증거를 보았지만

엄지발가락이 뜨거워지도록 걷다 보면
다른 계절을 만날 수 있을거야

살살이꽃

나 좀 봐,
너는 스쳐가는 바람이야?
가을 하늘 담느라 눈은 커졌는데
내 이름 한 번 안불러 주니
힝!

대나무처럼

소금 뿌려 삭혀놓은
나의 언어들이여

땅의 기운 받아
부디 잘 익어가소서

헤테로토피아

폐허가 열리면
들어오려는 여운이 반짝이고
어울리지 않은 반란이 시작된다

내가 시를 쓰는 것처럼

2부

Chain of Laughter

Laughter, the apex predator, knows no foe.

It gulps down all the pain from life's struggles.

Smile Virus

Wanna catch it?
It's a stubborn gene,
makes even raindrops grin.

For drying out a heavy heart,
there's nothing quite like it.

Chimney's Laughter

Every time a scorching fire was lit in my chest,
Did a new wrinkle appear, one by one?

My father's cap,
Burning white the charcoal-dark secrets Of his inner world.

Laughter Blooms

At lunchtime, bright words spill out delightfully,
rolling to the end of the hallway, blooming radiantly.

So much that adults can't even truly grasp it,
not even with the back of their ears.

Misjudgment

They deem me merely loud, like an empty can,
That I'm dressed in rags, A yawning rag, they scoffed.

Unaware my whole world is blooming with flowers.

April's Sky Lanterns

Embraced for so long,

Wept for so long.

Samrangjin Iron Bridge

Thirty li road, leading an ox, My father,
whose legs were like steel sinews.

Even leaning on his cane,
He never stopped in the end,
And crossed that entire river.

Spring's Arduous Tilling Flower

They say if the spring greens wither, her heart too dries up.
Mother, back bent from tirelessly tilling the land until it aches,
Resolutely, she performs 'hot plowing' even on mere scraps.

Mother's Spring

Your words, which cleansed even sorrow with priming water,

now pour down like cool midsummer water.

The Alley's Temperature

The sun's been down forever, why arn't you here for dinner?
　Mother's scolding voice, clinging to the alley wall.
　　As the wall's height seemed to shrink (to my grown eyes)
　　　So too, the warmth of people was cooling.

On a Rainy Spring Day

While raindrops linger,
The world is an aquarium.

The umbrella knows the sorrow of its tilt.

At the end of the spring day you left,
Drops fall even within me.

Alzheimer's

As I've lived, my memory often falters.
I've journeyed through countless paths.
It feels like I exchanged an old house for a new one,
But it certainly wasn't a smooth, easy road.

Commemorative Photo

On this gaunt face,
autumn wrinkles are deepening.

Through thunder and lightning,
I lived without batting an eye.
And yet, here I am.

Beautiful Drunken Reverie

Arise, my friend,
The stars have faded, it's dawn

Even if we drink through the night,
The sorrow that dampens your soul,
Can it truly be appeased?

Autobiography of an Ornamental Tree

Did I sprout new shoots, perhaps to console you?
I hope you'll take me into your eyes,
and read even the chill within my core.
I stand, like a proverb on a bookshelf.

Chaeseokgang

Until my joints creaked,
I bolted the door.
Yet, what can I do about
the inner feelings that still show?

The sea, truly⋯

Song of the Waves

When countless stories accumulate on the sand,
The sea extends its brine-soaked lines, in postcard style.

The song, folded in half, holds spaces so deep and wide,
That gulls, reading with their ears, sing along with the waves.

The Speed of Prayer

To sew each button of scarcity, one by one,
is to dress oneself with fervent longing.
Thus, my prayer is slow,
yet it never ceases.

Footprint

With the heel of time,
Did you engrave a single name?

To show that here, you
Breathed and loved,
And played to your heart's content.

The Allure of the Cherry Blossom

Oh, what am I to do?
In spring, you made my heart flutter with flower petals,
Then, in autumn, you wore the sky, sewn together,
Dropping a single button,
And there, your silhouette, translucent within.

Coordinates of Spring

The moment swans and mathematics meet,
A small world, made coordinates by rows and columns.

When winter is stirred,
Waves spread out by multiplication,
That very spot where wings must powerfully beat.

A Certain Reconciliation

How stubbornly they must have fought,
that Spring, unable to watch any longer,

    to winter and winter,
    urges reconciliation.

Superego

Enduring centuries of wind,
Etching the seasons' knots,

A temple settled in its core,

Gripping secrets deep within the earth,
It lives on, even in death.

Spring's Stirrings

A solitary green pine,
Spring, a tickle in its depths.

In the light pink flower-wind,
All its pinecones will be lost.

Monologue

Listen, friend,
Even in a place where no one treads, it's not desolate.

The empty spaces are filled by the sunlight,
The wall shields my cold knees,

And the wind thoughtfully brings tidings of the world.

The Struggle

If you keep whining about just stepping over
a single railroad tie,

even heaven will feel like hell to you.

The Roe Deer's Halt

Deficiency builds a nest even in the void,
A house of sorrow, mended as if intertwined and set aside,
Bearing a day's worth of muscle, tightly bound.

A conduit's life

A hot head,
A cold heart,
The way a Yes-man somehow lives as such

Upper Limit Yearning

Desire, sweet, grows to the crown of my head,
Yet no hot, red pillar ever soared.
Pressing my thumb as if chased,
Only a raw, blue-green bruise remained.
Ah, an unreachable mirage.

Angina

Even if it's an ordeal
that makes you clutch your neck,
as if veins might burst forth,

you must not utter words of rage.

Even if you swell as if to explode,
the sky has opened, you see.

The Old Soldier of Ssamjitgol

Though his body has aged,
And he lies beneath a vivid blue blanket,
The spirit to soar through the vast sky,
And his audacity to pierce through the clouds,
Still remain undiminished.

White-Haired Youth

Though time, like snow, has settled heavily,
Let's not begrudge the green of seasons past.

On the nape of a slumbering lake,
Let's skip stones, and draw forth spring.

I'm Sorry

I've lied for thirty years,
promising to change next spring,
and not to just make do with a mere grass ring.

Wind Wall

A wife who turns her back, speaking only to herself,
A husband who demands that she pinpoint his mistakes.

To dismantle what is unseen,
It takes courage to face it.

Together

Honey, the sun is setting.
What does it matter, when we're together⋯

The stooped twilight
is profoundly eavesdropping.

Counteraction

When you draw near, I ache.

With every slap,
I crumple like a canvas battered by a brush-whip.
I erect a cliff, transforming my face.

Yielding when you ask, enduring when you push away.

Couple

When the wind bites fierce,
You are the dense snow blossoms.
When darkness is indifferent,
You are the consoling starlight.
The one who embraces me with such warmth.

The Legend of the Couple Pine Tree

Bewitched by the festive music whispered by the rice ears,
The ferryman couple stepped into the painting.
No matter how much they rowed, they couldn't move forward,
And so, they became trees, anchored in the golden fields.

First Love

Love is gathering sunlight.
The moment we meet,
I want to open my whole self.

Newlywed

Before we even spread the blanket,
A feeling overflows,
As pure and soft as the first snow.

Lost in fluffy thoughts,
While we stay awake all night

Menopause

Did you grieve, having lost the familiar yesterday?
A sudden heat, arriving at the twilight of crimson days.

Having polished and nurtured two stars, shining like mirrors,
It's merely an unfamiliar labor, to find yourself again.

Same Day, Same Hour

Was it merely a fleeting wish?

The memory of sharing sunlight,
Crouched by the wall, still shines so brilliantly,

Yet I, lingering a little longer,
Am still here.

Breath

Even if I became a mountain, lying with punctured lungs,
At the end of each breath exhaled, there were the intertwined prayers of my wife and children.

Even if I hid my true feelings, going back and forth to the mine's deepest pit under the black sky,
I warmed the warmest spot of the floor with my hot heart.

Listening

Festering for eons,
The single word that gushes forth,

Crash!

A Backward Arrow

In a place where you've lost your way,
When you don't know which path to take,

Rather than a stubborn arrowhead,
Even if tangled, like a water droplet.

The Dooly I Met

In the tunnel,
there were days I fumbled through.
I hadn't known until then
that there was a light within me.

Adding a Footnote to "The Highest Good is Like Water"*

Remaining in the lowest place,
Shall we flow like water?

Or for the high places with a beast's face,
Shall we confront them with wide-open eyes?

*A four-character idiom from Chapter 8 of Laozi's Tao Te Ching

The River of Ideologies

I, towards the sun's east,
You, towards the wind's west.

Though bound by the fins of time,
When the water flows in, we journey as one.

Legacy

I've sprouted as much as I could,
And borne as much fruit as I could.
The purpose of a life lived, full of toil and trouble,
I leave behind as a legacy.

Forgiveness

How could it be easy?
That stone that sealed my words,
If you just let it drop,

Even a pathless road,
They say, becomes a path.

How to Savor Winter

When my appetite is frozen stiff,
And the day it thaws feels so far off,

I coat it thickly with pure white snow powder,
And fry it savory in the low-temperature sunlight.

.

How about it, does it look delicious

My Territory

A tiny patch of garden in a secluded rest stop,
I must stand guard, my beard bristling high.
For I am the king.

You may just hurry on by

Flying Youth

You shine in your own way.

Just take flight.

Everlasting Affection

Where her hand reaches for a meal,
It's a place where even their eyes are sated.

Because love is something held in the gaze,
Even while eating, they only look at Mom.

Adolescence

Where did the child, once meek as a lamb, go?

"You should study," I say.
"I'm about to,
why are you like this?" they retort.

What's outside the fence that they only gaze in that direction?

Impatient Technology

What should I do?
Though the day will come
When it rolls on the ground and flies in the sky,
If you already lift it up like this

Guardian

Hey, Mr. Shin,
The fireworks festival is in full swing in the back neighborhood,

But with your red eyes wide open,
You stay up all night guarding the village.
Thank you for your hard work.

You Tube

I wish what's told all over town
    Were true.

Like the wind's tongue
Caressing the stretched-out twilight,

Not False, But True.

Job seeker

I sensed the coming blizzard,
saw the ground's silent proof.

But if I walk until my big toe burns,
I'm sure to find another season.

Salsal-i Flower (Cosmos)

Hey, look at me,
Are you just a passing breeze?
My eyes grew wide, trying to capture the autumn sky,
But you won't even call my name once?
Hmph!

Like bamboo,

Oh, my words,
salted and matured,

Receiving the earth's vigor,
May you ripen beautifully.

Heterotopia

When ruins open,
Lingering traces glisten, seeking entry,
An unfitting rebellion begins,

Just like I write poetry.

숨

2025년 8월 11일 초판 1쇄 찍음
2025년 8월 20일 초판 1쇄 펴냄

지은이 _ 장 훈
펴낸이 _ 라문석
편집장 _ 김옥경
디자인 _ 장상호

펴 낸 곳 _ 도서출판 두엄
등록번호 _ 제03-01-503호
주　　소 _ (41969) 대구광역시 중구 명륜로12길 21
대표전화 _ (053) 423-2214
전자우편 _ dueum@hanmail.net

ⓒ장훈, 2025
ISBN 979-11-93360-25-5 03810

* 지은이와 협의하여 인지는 생략합니다.
* 이 책 내용의 전부 또는 일부를 재사용하려면 반드시 지은이와
  도서출판 두엄 양측의 동의를 받아야 합니다.
* 책값은 뒤표지에 표시되어 있습니다.